Alfred Nevin

Words of Comfort for Doubting Hearts

Alfred Nevin

Words of Comfort for Doubting Hearts

ISBN/EAN: 9783744735933

Printed in Europe, USA, Canada, Australia, Japan

Cover: Foto ©Thomas Meinert / pixelio.de

More available books at **www.hansebooks.com**

Words of Comfort

FOR

Doubting Hearts.

BY

ALFRED NEVIN, D.D.

Whereby shall I know that I shall inherit it?—Gen. xv. 8.

A bruised reed shall he not break, and smoking flax shall he not quench.—Matt. xii. 20.

For he that is not against us is on our part.—Mark ix. 40.

NEW YORK:
Anson D. F. Randolph,
770 Broadway.
1867.

Entered according to Act of Congress, in the year 1867,

By ANSON D. F. RANDOLPH,

In the Clerk's Office of the District Court of the U. S. for the Southern District of New York.

E. O. JENKINS, PRINTER AND STEREOTYPER,
20 NORTH WILLIAM ST., N. Y.

"Two things may quiet any man's conscience under the greatest guilt. 1. Is there not a sufficient sacrifice? Is there not satisfaction and atonement in the blood of Christ? Is not this a sufficient sacrifice? 2. Is it thine? This I know unbelief is apt to stagger at, but do but lay the hand of thy faith upon the head of the sacrifice, and confess and forsake thy sins, and all that Christ hath done shall be as effectual for thy good as if thou thyself hadst suffered, yea, infinitely more."—*Mather.*

"We cannot expect spiritual thoughts and affections from truths which are but imperfectly understood, or doubtfully and feebly believed."—*J. A. James.*

"Satan, in his temptations, strikes principally at the *faith* of God's people, that being the grace which gives most glory to God, and in the exercise of which believers have much peace, joy and comfort; and it is also a shield which keeps off and quenches his fiery darts, and therefore he endeavors all he can to weaken and destroy it, or wrest it out of their hands."—*Dr. Gill.*

"When we look at our great High Priest in faith, we may look at ourselves (bad as we are) without despair, at our enemies (however many) without fear, at our trials (however great) without repining, and at our duties (however difficult) without discouragement."—*Cox.*

"Sinners can do nothing but make wounds that Christ may heal them, and make debts that He may pay them, and make falls that He may raise them, and make deaths that He may quicken them, and spin out and dig hells for themselves that He may ransom them. Now I will bless the Lord that ever there was such a thing as the free grace of God, and a free ransom given for sold souls: only, alas! guiltiness maketh me ashamed to apply to Christ, and to think it pride in me to put out my unclean and withered hand to such a Saviour! But it is neither shame nor pride for a drowning man to swim to a rock, nor for a ship-broken soul to run himself ashore upon Christ."— *Rutherford.*

"Cling to the Crucified:
His death is life to thee—
Life for eternity!
His pains thy pardon seal;
His stripes thy bruises heal,
His cross proclaims thy peace,
Bids every sorrow cease.
His blood is all to thee,
It purges thee from sin;
It sets thy spirit free,
It keeps thy conscience clean,
Cling to the Crucified!

"Cling to the Crucified:
His is a heart of love,
Full as the hearts above,
Its depths of sympathy
Are all awake for thee.
His countenance is light,
Even in the darkest night.
That love shall never change,
That light shall ne'er grow dim.
Change thou thy faithless heart
To find its all in Him.
Cling to the Crucified!"

COMFORTING WORDS.

NO NEUTRALITY IN RELIGION

No one can occupy an intermediate point between the friends and the enemies of God. Every human being, in the possession of a sound mind, is either a saint or a sinner, either penitent or impenitent, either a believer or an unbeliever. It is true that shades of character are so blended in the Church and in the world, that it is difficult, if at all possible, to determine precisely the line of distinction between them; but it is also and equally true, that every intelligent being is marked by conformity to the will of God, or the want of it.

This is necessarily so from the very constitution of our nature. Man was not made to be neutral in regard to anything, nor can he be. He was made to feel, and feel he must and does in relation to every object that attracts his attention or affects his interest. His heart, like the pendulum in its oscillation, is constantly moving from attachment to aversion, from hope to fear, and from approbation to condemnation, or in the opposite direction. And what is true of him in regard to matters of limited and transient importance is, of course, much more so in regard to religion. Here the interests involved are transcendently great. They are high as heaven, deep as hell. Hence it is utterly impossible for us to be brought, as we all are, in contact with this system, without taking a position either friendly or hostile to it. It is to affect us so deeply, so much and so long, that we are forced to form an opinion touching it, either favorable or adverse. This is what Jesus meant in saying, "He tnat is not with me is against me." So long as men possess any moral character, they must view themselves, and be regarded by others, as either for God or against him. In the great contest which enlists the feelings and the power of three worlds, it is impossible that there should be a neutral. One side or the other will claim, and does claim, every rational being in heaven and on earth.

IS IT POSSIBLE TO BE A CHRISTIAN WITHOUT KNOWING IT?

It is beyond question that there are many persons who exhibit the fruits of personal piety, and yet are not satisfied that they are the children of God. Such persons, though free from all doubts of the divine origin of Christianity, and thoroughly persuaded of the importance of an interest in the great salvation, and walking unblamably in the commandments of the Lord, yet are unable to decide, to their own satisfaction, whether they have found the " pearl of great price." They are not sure that they have been received into the household of faith. Sometimes they think they belong to it; then, again, they think or fear they do not. They are vexed and oppressed with doubts on what, to them, is the weightiest of all problems. From the depths of an aching heart they are constrained to say:

> " 'Tis a point I long to know,
> Oft it gives me anxious thought,
> Do I love the Lord, or no,
> Am I his, or am I not?"

They are afraid that they are only informed, but not enlightened, only convinced, not converted, only *almost*, not *altogether*, Christians. Their solicitude is deepened by their consciousness of the deceitfulness of their hearts, as well as by the revealed possibility that presumptions or persuasions may be cherished which may outlive the pang of dying, and knock at the very gate of heaven, only that their deluded victim may be repulsed by the Master's word, *I never knew you.*

Oh, how painful is such uncertainty! How many dark shadows does it cast over the pathway of life! And how vain the attempt to remove it, by having recourse to such unreasonable and unreliable sources of evidence as accidental occurrences, visions, dreams, and sudden impulses!

Dear reader, assuming that you belong to the class of persons just described, I undertake, with such strength as God may impart, to assist you in settling to your comfort, if not even to your joy, the question which gives you so much concern. I propose to defend your faint, wavering hope of salvation against the doubts and fears which assail it. And in order that your mind may be prepared to appreciate the evidence of Christian character which shall be presented, I ask you, in advance, to ponder carefully and prayerfully certain propositions which I shall state, and all of which bear with more or less force and directness on the momentous issues to be decided.

THE TIME, PLACE, AND MODE OF REGENERATION NEED NOT BE KNOWN

A MAN may be a Christian without being able to tell when, where, or how he was born again. On these points the experience of the true disciples of Jesus is very different. Some can tell the time of their conversion, giving day and date, the hour, the providence, the place, the text, the preacher, and all the circumstances connected with it. They can show the word that penetrated their soul, and in some truths of Scripture the salve that healed the sore, the balm that stanched the blood, and the bandage that Christ's own hand wrapped on the bleeding wound. It is not so, however, with all, or, perhaps, with most Christians.

We turn our face to the east and our back to the setting stars, to note the very moment of the birth of morning, yet we cannot tell when and where the first faint, cold, steel-gray gleam appears. Thus, too, if our eyes are fixed upon the earth, both night and day, so silently does the green blade come forth from the bosom of the earth, and so gradually does it show itself, that we could not possibly determine the exact moment when it appeared. Now, as it is with morning's birth, so is it with many in relation to their spiritual dawn; both are marked by faint and feeble streaks of light, yet both shine more and more unto the perfect day. And as the green blade springs up silently and gradually from the virgin soil, so, with noiseless steps, divine mercy comes to the sinner's heart to make way for the sinner's Friend, and gently, oftentimes, the hand of love removes our chains, and softly does the dew of heaven steal into the heart, to cause the seed of truth to germinate and grow. .

Just, therefore, as the husbandman refuses not to rejoice as he beholds the growing corn, because he cannot tell the time when it pierced the sod; and as the mariner refuses not to recognize the grateful light which shines around him, because he could not decide just when night gave place to day; so neither need any one be perplexed because he cannot tell the precise hour when the Omnipotent finger of God's grace first touched his heart—the first dew-drop of heaven's mercy distilled upon his spirit. "The way of the Spirit of God," says an old writer, " is always undiscernible to flesh and blood. The soul receives a thing, and the man knows not how ; he can (scarce possibly, not at all) tell where, by whom, or which way it came to him, it was brought, and with a most blessed, *gracious sleight-of-hand conveyed into his heart.*"

NO DEGREE OF FAITH, IF IT IS TRUE AND LIVING FAITH, IS TOO SMALL FOR THE PURPOSE OF SALVATION

Even the disciples who were in the vessel with Jesus, during the storm on the Sea of Galilee, possessed but little faith. The ship-wrecked sailor, if he has been cast upon a rock but a single foot above the reach of the waves, is as perfectly secure as if he were looking down from a thousand fathoms upon the troubled waters. So, if by Divine grace any soul has really found a resting-place upon the Rock of Ages, God will not despise the day of small things—the disciple of little faith.

There is a difference among the Lord's people. There are not only sheep, but lambs. There are babes, and little children, as well as young men, and those of full age, who have their senses exercised, by reason of use, to discern both good and evil. The seed of the Gospel, which has been made to take root in the heart, brings forth unequally; in some, thirty, in some, sixty, and in some, an hundred fold. This difference should be well marked by weak believers. Such persons are constantly tempted to an undervaluation of what God has done for them. Comparing themselves with others who are more advanced in the Divine life, they naturally have a strong inclination to shrink into nothing, and imagine that they have no part or lot in the matter. But why should such inclination be indulged? When we look into the Bible, do we not learn that the work of grace in the soul is generally small, resembling the field where the blade precedes the ear,—that the Christian is a soldier, who at first is a raw and awkward recruit, neither marching well, nor easily and gracefully using his arms,—that he is a scholar, who, on entering the school, begins with his rudiments, and, though he has many things to learn, "cannot bear them now"—and that the man whose faith is but as a grain of mustard-seed, is interested in all the promises of the Gospel, a child of God, and a joint-heir with Christ of the heavenly inheritance? With such a representation, therefore, no man should despise his own measure of piety, inconsiderable though it may be in comparison with that of others. Rather should he be thankful if he has only light enough to see his darkness, and feeling enough to be sensible of his obduracy.

> "Cold as I feel this heart of mine,
> Yet, since I *feel* it so,
> It yields some hope of life divine
> Within, however low."

It is his duty to cherish the degree of grace which he has received, and to seek to have it increased by more fervent prayer, more frequent and intimate communion with Jesus, and, above all, by conscientiously and consistently acting according to that portion of light which God has given him. The truth is, that no surer method could be adopted by any one to destroy within him every evidence of piety, than making little account of the measure of grace that has been given to him,—no surer method, either of shutting the ear and hand of

God against him, than placing a low estimate upon the blessings he has received, and murmuring because he has not received more. "To him that hath shall be given."

THE INFLUENCE OF PHYSICAL CAUSES MUST BE CONSIDERED IN JUDGING OF CHRISTIAN CHARACTER.

We are "fearfully and wonderfully made." The mind and the body are very nearly related, and are subject to constant and powerful interaction. It is almost impossible for one to be to any considerable degree affected, without the other being brought into sympathy with it. It is unnecessary to adduce proof of this proposition, as every one knows it to be true from his own consciousness and observation. When the friends of Cowper requested him to prepare some hymns for the Olney Collection, he replied, "How can you ask of me such a service? I seem to myself to be banished to a remoteness from God's presence, in comparison with which the distance from East to West, is vicinity; is cohesion." There were other periods in the history of this good man, to whom the Church is indebted for that sweet hymn, "Oh, for a closer walk with God," and many others as richly fraught with spirituality, when he seemed to be abandoned to the darkest gloom, if not to actual despair, in respect to his religious state. That this sad experience was mainly, if not solely, ascribable to the variableness of his health, no one, perhaps, has ever doubted, who has made himself acquainted with his profound devotional tastes and habits, his exemplary life, and his delicate and peculiar physical organization.

MODIFYING POWER OF TEMPERAMENT.

It is undeniable that temperament considerably modifies piety. As water is dependent, in some degree, for its color and taste, on the nature of the soil over which it flows, so personal religion takes its complexion somewhat from the disposition of the individual in whose heart it has found a place. "There is one Spirit, but a diversity of operations." Grace, though it corrects, does not eradicate nature.

It is true that "if any man be in Christ, he is a new creature," but he is not a new creature in such a sense that he has lost his personal identity. Christianity does not aim to re-construct its subjects, but only to sanctify them. Neither does it seek to bring them into complete resemblance to one another. Whilst it does produce a community of saints, one faith, one love, one hope, the same humility and self-denial in all the members of the Church, it does not propose to produce identity of thought, temper of mind and inclination. The man, therefore, who has experienced its renovating power, is neither physically, nor intellectually, nor socially changed. The same thing is true of his natural temperament, whether it was before his regeneration phlegmatic, sanguine, choleric, or melancholic, it continues the same. The only difference in his case after the new birth, is, that a new and powerful principle has been introduced into his soul, which gives a new control and direction to his nature, making him to live under the mastery of new motives, and for new ends. In other words, regeneration is not destroying the metal, but the old stamp upon it, to imprint a new one. It is not breaking the candlestick, but putting a new light in it. It is a new stringing of the instrument, to make new harmony. For example, " Divine grace did not give John his warm affections, but it fixed them on his beloved Master—sanctifying his love. It did not inspire Nehemiah with the love of country, but it made him a holy patriot. It did not give Dorcas a woman's heart, her tender sympathy with suffering, but it associated charity with piety, and made her a holy philanthropist. It did not give Paul his vehemence and energy of character, his genius, his resistless logic, and noble oratory, but it consecrated them to the cause of Christ; touching his lips with a live coal from the altar, it made him such a master of holy eloquence that he swayed the multitude at his will, humbled the pride of kings, and compelled his very judges to tremble. It did not give David a poet's fire and a poet's lyre, but it strung his harp with chords from heaven, and tuned all its strings to the service of religion and the high praises of God."

Referring now more particularly to difference of temperament, we point to the Sisters of Bethany for an illustration. Martha, as the narrative shows, was active, energetic, decided, but Mary was quiet, pensive and meditative. These traits of character were brought out during the visit of Jesus, when the one was reproved for being "careful and troubled about many things," and the other was commended for having "chosen the good part." "Here were two persons, born of the same parents, reared under the same educational influences, and yet widely variant in their dispositions. That *both* were Christians, notwithstanding the rebuke which one received on account of the triumph of domestic vanity at the time, admits not of a doubt, yet their piety did not produce an entire assimilation of their tastes and habits. It shows itself by different manifestations. The one was of a free, bustling spirit, inclined to interest herself in household affairs, and make her presence felt in the sphere she occupied; the other was disposed to seclusion and reflection, yet Divine grace was lodged in the heart of each, and was preparing both for heaven.

Just at this point it may be proper to say, that the temperament of any one has much to do with the form of his experience at his very introduction to the life of faith. The Holy Spirit, the author of regeneration, moves on the soul, not in any way set down and arranged, so that man can follow and trace this out, but absolutely independent of all such set and appointed ways. He moveth as He "listeth," or as it may please Him. He is not tied to the preaching of the Gospel, nor to the reading of the

Bible, nor to the strange and wondrous providences which befall man, nor to ordinances, not even to Baptism or to that of the Lord's Supper. Neither does He confine himself to any particular type or formula of operation in bringing sinners into a saving relation to God. When Jesus approached Matthew as he sat at the receipt of custom, and addressed to him these few and simple words, "Follow me," without the hesitation of a moment, without the reply of a word, the publican arose, and leaving all in which he had been a moment before immersed, instantly obeyed the summons, and from that hour, through good and ill, through toil and labor, through persecution and privation, through contempt, reproach and infamy, he followed the Saviour of the world. Wonderful illustration of the truth of this declaration of our Lord, "My sheep hear my voice, and I know them, and they follow me." When Lydia sat by the river's side, among the hearers of Paul, as he proclaimed the Gospel, the Lord opened her heart to receive the things that were spoken, as gently as a rose-bud is unfolded by the rays of the morning sun. The Philippian jailor came to the incarcerated Apostles, trembling, falling down before them, and with most earnest emphasis asking, "Sirs, what must I do to be saved?"— thus indicating that his soul was experiencing a convulsion corresponding with the earthquake that shook the prison to its foundations—yet this was God's plan of bringing *him* to believe in the Lord Jesus Christ, that peace might dawn upon his agitated spirit, and an interest in the everlasting covenant of mercy be secured.

Thus is it true that there is no uniform method by which God brings sinners to Himself. Some are instantly brought into a gracious state, others are kept long seeking for the desired renovation. Some are deeply exercised with sorrow, and then with joy, others have comparatively little emotion. "Sometimes," says *Caryl*, " truth enters in *state*, and it may be said to make its passage visibly into the heart of the man. The word comes not as a company of thieves, but as a band of soldiers, with weapons drawn, and terrible shouts, tearing open the soul and breaking open the iron gate of the heart, locked and barred by unbelief, to secure that cursed crew of lusts garrisoned within it. The weapons of our warfare (saith the apostle) are mighty through God; the Word is mighty, wonderful in strength; it comes upon the soul as an armed man, to spoil it of all sinful treasures; yea, of the very life of sin. Sometimes the Lord proclaimed war, as by an herald of arms, against a man, and openly prepared for his siege and battery. *He surprises another, and steals him into a happy captivity to Himself.*"

It is, therefore, unwarranted and unwise, for any one to decide that he has not passed from death to life, merely because he has not had the same degree of conviction of sin and of spiritual struggle which others have had in making this great transition. Equally so is it for any one to conclude that he has no piety, because his character in its developments is not precisely identical with that of others whom he regards as Christians. What inference must the loving and retiring John have drawn concerning his interest in the scheme of salvation, if he had judged himself by comparison with the fiery and forward Peter? Or how could the bold Luther have retained his hope of heaven, if he could not believe any one to be a Christian, unless he was like the gentle Melancthou? Each individual should remember his own peculiarities of temperament and disposition, in judging of his religion. One of the not least important of the peculiarities of many persons, is a tendency to take gloomy views of themselves. They look with a doubting or distrustful eye on everything that pertains to them, and this feeling pervades the sphere of their spiritual interests. Nothing of a worldly kind which they have is deemed as good as what their neighbors have, and soon, and for the same reason, their piety is regarded not only as inferior, but also as unreal. They write bitter things against themselves. They go through life, seeing only the dark side of the pillar-cloud, which leads God's people through this wilderness to the promised inheritance. And with such a tendency, how strong, how fearful the probability that they may dishonor God by questioning the good work which He may have begun within them!

The fact is, no general law can be laid down for the operation of God's Spirit upon the feelings. It is, to carry out the Saviour's own figure, like the action of the wind upon different trees and shrubs. The same breeze blows upon the poplar, and it shivers and trembles and turns its silvery leaves to the light, looking as if some magic had blanched its verdure. It blows upon the elm, and it slowly and gracefully swings its heavy tassels. Upon the pine, and it sways majestically and sings mournfully. Upon the rose, and it shakes and showers its tinted leaves upon the ground. The action of the same wind is modified by the structure of each different tree or plant. So conviction of sin will affect differently each one of a dozen of men. Two men lose each a child. The funerals are on the same day. We go into the house of one, and find him standing over the little coffin, trembling in every limb, his sobs coming thick and fast, and calling his child's name in tones of the bitterest anguish. We repair to the other's house. He sits calmly by his dead, not a tear in his eye. He speaks to us in his accustomed tone about his child. He asks if our own little ones are well. Now, will we go and tell our friends that the latter is a man of no feeling, and that he does not seem at all affected by his loss? Do we not, on the contrary, ascribe to him a grief as sincere as his neighbor's? Do we not know that the quiet, self-contained man is often the keener sufferer of the two?

So, dear reader, you are not to doubt the reality of your repentance because it is not precisely similar to that of your friend or neighbor. He may have been harassed, horrified, overwhelmed by the view of his sinful state. He may fill the nights with weeping and forget to eat his bread. You, on the contrary, may just as clearly have discerned your relations to God, hated sin as intensely, and longed as earnestly to escape from it, yet with you it may have been rather a matter of judgment than of feeling. The same conviction manifests itself in both, through your natural differences of temperament and character, as the same light shines through different colored panes. It would be well for you to remember that if your sense of sinfulness produced in you a degree of emotion bordering on frenzy, and did not bring you to Jesus, it would be spurious repentance; and, on the contrary, if your feelings were calm as a summer sea, and yet brought you to the Cross with confession and submission, nothing more would be necessary. Jesus asks nothing more.

"All the fitness He requireth
Is to feel your need of Him."

ASSURANCE IS NOT ESSENTIAL TO SALVATION.

There are two kinds or forms of assurance. The one is called the *assurance of faith*, the other, the *assurance of hope*, and, sometimes, the full assurance of hope. (Heb. vi. 2.) As faith unfolds into hope, so the assurance or highest measure of faith into the assurance or highest measure of hope. They therefore often co-exist.

"The Assurance of Faith," says an eminent divine, "is the acme of unwavering and undoubting confidence that the propositions of revealed truth are the very truth of God,—a persuasion so firm, as to be the basis and resting-place of all Christian reliance. It is saving faith carried to its height. It sees Christ, and believes in him. The Assurance of Hope is a settled, unshaken, well-grounded, immovable persuasion, and certainty, that I, as an individual, have thus believed, that I am in Christ, that God is my reconciled Father, that I shall never come into condemnation, and that my heaven is secure. The former is an universal duty, the latter is a gracious privilege. One is possessed by every believer, the other is a sovereign gift to a part of the flock. By one, I believe that God is true, by the other, that he is my God. By the one, I see Christ to be an Almighty and a willing Saviour, by the other I am assured that He will save me in particular. By one, I lean on Christ as my only and all-sufficient supporter; by the other, I am made certain that I have actually done so, and hope without wavering that I shall eternally rejoice in him. One is opposed to unbelief; the other, to despondency. One connects with Christ, the other reveals the connection. They stand to one another as the blossom to the fruit, or as the deed to the possession, or as the sentence of acquittal to enlargement from restraint. One may co-exist with many fears, the other casteth out all fear. 'The work of righteousness shall be peace, and the effect of righteousness, quietness and assurance forever.'

"Is assurance of personal salvation essential to saving faith? Some have maintained the affirmative and have taught that no man can be a regenerate person without knowing himself to be such. But the negative is clearly the doctrine of Scripture. Bearing in mind the distinction already suggested, between the Assurance of Faith and the Assurance of Hope, it will readily be perceived that one may have a justifying faith without any necessary reference to the question, whether he is himself regenerate or not. And, inasmuch as any, the least degree of faith, is justifying, as uniting the soul to Christ, it will as readily be perceived that faith may apprehend Christ when as yet it falls far short of that which produces assured hope."

That assurance is eminently desirable, requires no proof. It is impossible, indeed, to value too highly the privilege of a conscious interest in the favor of God, and no one who is not indifferent to the highest happiness that can be enjoyed on earth, will fail to seek after this privilege. Still, it is true, that it is not by assurance, but by faith, that we are saved. "He that believeth shall be saved." Assurance is a fruit of faith, and as such it frequently does not grow until the principle from which it springs has been long and largely exercised. We are aware that some maintain that it is impossible for a man to believe without knowing that he does so, but this is not true. Faith does not necessarily carry with it self-evidencing power, else why would the Apostle have said to the Corinthians, " examine yourselves whether ye be in the faith," and, " prove your own selves?" These injunctions certainly at least imply, that faith does not of itself prove its existence, and that it may, as a principle, be lodged in the heart when there is not a full realization of its presence.

And who has not met with exemplifications of this truth? Again and again are those to be found whose lives furnish a beautiful illustration of the obedience of the Gospel, and yet they do not, nor can they, be persuaded to regard themselves as Christians. How is this? Here are the external evidences, and shall we doubt whether the Holy Spirit, *the sound whereof we hear* in these outward manifestations of fidelity, has implanted the vital power of godliness underneath or back of them? Can grapes grow on thorns, or figs on thistles? The only conclusion it seems to us possible to reach in these cases, is, that such persons really belong to the people of God, and that this relation is not at all invalidated by their want of assurance, inasmuch as such want arises from their deep humility, their fear of thinking too favorably of themselves, and the very high conception they have of what is involved in being a child of God and an heir of the kingdom of heaven. The last two of these reasons, it is to be believed, operate frequently and potently to prevent the enjoyment of Christian hope. Anxiety about any interest results from an appreciation of its importance. Instead of being true that it is easy to believe what we wish, in proportion as we love and value a thing we become the more apprehensive, and require every kind of proof and assurance concerning its safety. This apprehensiveness, with many who sit in judgment on their claims to everlasting life, shadows the faith that otherwise might be clear and strong. The great and good *Chalmers* said that he could without difficulty have persuaded himself of having a title to heaven, if the inheritance was not so vast,—utterly exceeding all his capacity to comprehend it, and he also recorded in his diary, that the passage of Scripture which most aptly represented his habitual religious experience was this :— " My heart breaketh for the longing it continually hath unto thy judgments."

We now come to the consideration of some tests, which may, under God's blessing, serve to show you, dear reader, whether you have only a name to live, and are dead, or are a genuine disciple of Jesus, sprinkled with his blood, born again by his Spirit, and moving on, though it be by a way which you know not, to the city whose walls shall never crumble, whose melodies shall never be hushed, and whose lustres shall never grow dim.

AN ENCOURAGING SIGN.

Is it not true, as at the beginning we have assumed, that you are earnestly desirous of knowing whether you are a Christian, and of becoming one, if you are not? If so, this very state of mind furnishes a strong argument in your favor. Anxiety on this subject is not likely to exist in a heart with which grace has had nothing to do. The time was when you had but little concern in regard to your spiritual condition and prospects. Such is not your feeling now, and this is a very encouraging indication. It at least shows that in your case the apathy of the carnal mind has been broken up, and profound interest has taken the place of cold indifference toward the things invisible and everlasting.

Bishop Hall remarked two centuries and a half ago, "If God had not said, 'Blessed are those that hunger,' I know not what could keep weak Christians from sinking in despair. Many times, all I can do is, to complain that I want Him and wish to recover Him." Does not this language express your experience? Are you not prepared to say as did Job,— 'Oh that I knew where I might find Him?" Do you not desire, above everything else, to stand in the favor, friendship and fellowship of God? Is not this desire so intense as to be aptly represented by the sensations of hunger and thirst? Do you not mourn over your lack of consciousness that God is your portion, and that you are so very little like Him in heart and life? Then take the comfort which the Saviour's words are adapted, and were designed, to convey,—" Blessed are they that do hunger and thirst after righteousness, for they shall be filled."

When the Esquimaux, in this country, first obtained the Gospel according to Matthew, in their own language, we are told, they perused the sacred treasure with the greatest attention. One day the Missionary found a poor lad weeping bitterly. He inquired the cause of his grief. The youth replied by pointing to this verse in the Sermon on the Mount,—" Blessed are the pure in heart, for they shall see God"—and then adding, " I am not pure, so I can never see him." " But stop," said the missionary, (placing his finger on the fourth verse,) " read again, ' Blessed are they that mourn, for they shall be comforted.' "

VIEWS OF SIN

Sin is the abominable thing which God hates. It is antagonistic to his character, law, government, plans, and it crucified his only-begotten and well-beloved Son. Standing before God in the relation of sinners, as all men do by nature and practice, there is a constant and fearful exposure on the part of every one to His wrath, as the threatened penalty for the " transgression of the law." Ordinarily, the sense of guilt which is connected with this relation is vague and feeble. But when the Holy Spirit convinces a man of his condemned and depraved condition, he sees, as he never saw before, that sin is an evil and a bitter thing. Is not this your experience? Can you not say, as did Paul, " I was alive without the law, but when the commandment came, sin revived, and I died?" Have you not, in the discovery which Divine illumination has given you of the deceitfulness and desperate wickedness of your heart, and of the purity and righteousness of God's law, been led to godly sorrow for your past ingratitude, rebellion and unbelief, especially under the light, goodness and mercy which should have constrained you to cherish a different spirit and pursue an opposite course? And have you not under a conviction of your ruined, wretched and helpless estate, looked with the eye of faith to Him who "is the end of the law for righteousness to every one that believeth?"

What, then, is there to prevent you having a good hope through grace? Do you answer, "I am conscious of so much sin yet dwelling in me that I cannot persuade myself I am a child of God?" To this I reply that a growing sense of inward corruption, instead of being evidence that you are not in a gracious state, is rather evidence that you are. Suppose a man in a dungeon abounding with noxious reptiles. While all is dark there, he sees none of them. The light *seems* to bring them and to multiply them, but it really only discovers what was there before. There are remains of evil in all the subjects of Divine grace. None of them are free. "In many things," says James, "we offend all." "My tears," said Bishop Beveridge, "require to be washed in the blood of Christ, and my repentance needs to be repented of."

Those who could die for the Saviour have used the most humbling language with regard to themselves. "Sometimes," said the pious Bradford, "O, my God, there seems to be no difference between me and the wicked, my understanding seems as dark as theirs, and my heart as hard as theirs." "Iniquities prevail against me," was the complaint of David. He did not say, iniquities prevail *with* me, but *against* me. As to many, they prevail *with* them. *They* drink in iniquity as the ox drinketh in water. *They* draw iniquity with cords of vanity. But a Christian is made willing in the day of God's power. and therefore can say, "To will is present with me, but how to perform that which is good, I find not. When I *would* do good, evil is present with me." What a difference is there between Ahab, who is said to have sold himself to work wickedness, and the poor slave in Africa, who, kidnapped, and disposed of to demon-traffickers in flesh and blood, though he resists and weeps, still finds those traffickers prevail *against* him? So, says Paul, I do not sell myself, but "I am sold under sin." So, then, "it is no more I that do it, but sin that dwelleth in me. O wretched man that I am! who shall deliver me from the body of this death?" What a representation is this of the sin that dwelleth even in God's dear people! It is, says one, as is commonly supposed, a reference to a cruel usage sometimes practised by the tyrants of antiquity, and which consisted in fastening a dead carcass to a living man. Body was bound to body—hands to hands, face to face, lips to lips. The living man could not separate himself from his hated companion; it lay down and rose up, and walked with him. He could not breathe without inhaling a kind of pestilence. Yet this representation, strong as it is, is not too strong to be true. Sin still cleaves to Christians till they are translated to glory. It is with them, when alone, and when in company, in the work of the field, the office, or the shop, and in the worship of the closet or the sanctuary. It is at once their burden and their grief. They have a new nature, and as *far* as they are sanctified, there is as perfect a contrariety between them and sin, as between darkness and light. Hence there is a contest within them, the flesh lusteth against the Spirit, and the Spirit against the flesh, these being contrary the one to the other. This very contest, however, is proof that the element of grace, filling them with abhorrence of sin, has been lodged in their hearts.

It is, therefore, no evidence that a man is not a Christian that inquities prevail against him. An enemy may make a temporary irruption into a country and do injury, but if he is soon expelled again, there is evidence that the power invaded has superior force. So if evil passions rise up in the heart, and are resisted and suppressed, there is proof that *grace reigns.* David, when uttering the complaint we have referred to a little before, could yet say in triumph,—" As for our transgressions, thou shalt purge them away." Paul, when mourning, as we have seen, over his indwelling corruption, could yet say, " I thank God through Jesus Christ our Lord." So may the weakest believer, if he will, under the deepest sense of his ill-desert, joy in God through our Lord Jesus Christ, by whom he has now received the atonement, and, with confidence and triumph, sing—

> "Thy Spirit holds perpetual war
> And wrestles and complains,
> But views the happy moment near
> That shall dissolve the chains."

THE PLAN OF SALVATION.

In order to be reconciled to God, it is necessary that we be justified. What is justification? It is often confounded with sanctification, but should not be. It is not the making us righteous in person, but in state. It stands opposed to *condemnation*. It is the absolving a man from a charge, the acquitting him, when accused, and pronouncing him righteous. "Justification regards something done *for* us; sanctification, something done *in* us. The one is a relative, the other a personal change. The one is a change in our state, the other in our nature. The one is perfect at once, the other is gradual. The one is derived from the obedience of the Saviour, the other from His Spirit. The one gives us a title to heaven, the other a meetness for it. Thus are they distinct, though always united."

That our justification as sinners before God is free, is beyond question. "We are justified freely by his grace, through the redemption that is in Christ Jesus, whom God has set forth as a propitiation for sin." Thus is it manifest that in dealing with God for his favor, we are not merchants, but suppliants. We cannot buy, but must beg. We have no merit to plead. As sinners, we have forfeited all expectation from God, except a "fearful looking for of judgment and fiery indignation." Hence if we obtain salvation, it can only be as a gratuity. This inestimable blessing can only be secured " by the faith of Christ." (Gal. ii. 16.) It is not necessary to be able to explain precisely how faith justifies the soul. It should be enough for us to know that it is a truth clearly revealed.

Now, what *is* faith? Is it a belief that Christ died for me in particular? I answer unhesitatingly, No. As previously remarked, the Bible teaches nothing like this. Indeed the highest and most seraphic form of faith may be so abused in the great object, Jesus Christ, as to lose all regard to self, or even its own salvation. "Saving faith is not a belief that I have saving faith, but a belief in Christ, the Saviour, and a receiving of Him as offered in the Word, a holding of the recorded offer to be credible, and a setting to the seal that God is true. The delightful inference, that I am a saved soul, may be true,— may follow logically from the truths believed, and my act of believing,—may, therefore, in some sort, be involved in the proposition, I believe, and yet it is no part of that faith which is saving. The Bible nowhere enjoins it as such. It is a happy fruit of faith. But some will ask, can so great a change take place without the subject being conscious of it? We answer, no. The subject is conscious, but something more is needed to assure him. He knows there is a change, but is it *the* change? It is asked, can it be possible for a prisoner to be loosed from such a bond without knowing it? We answer, Peter was released by an angel from prison, "and went out and followed him, and wist not that it was true which was done by the angel, but he thought he saw a vision." So it may be with the emancipated soul.

"Have you, then, dear reader, faith? Jesus Christ—"the gift of God," came into the world to save sinners in a way equally *gracious* and *holy*. Do you acquiesce in a purpose which involves the destruction of *self* and *sin?* Do you believe the record, that " God hath given unto us eternal life, and this life is in His Son ?" Have you received Christ as He is presented to us in the Word and means of grace? " Zaccheus made haste, and came down, and received Him joyfully." Did you ever give Him such a welcome? Have you received Him wholly—as your Prophet, King, Priest and Exemplar? Have you given yourself to Him? I mean not your substance only, or your time only, but *yourself*. Can you remember such a surrender,— an evening, perhaps, when, like Isaac in the field, you said, " Lord, I am thine, save me?" or, the close of a Sabbath, perhaps, when in your closet you read and wept, and kneeled, and then rose and wept and kneeled again, and said,

"O, Lord, other lords besides Thee have had dominion over me, henceforth by Thee only will I make mention of Thy Name?" Do you supremely prize the Saviour? He is precious to them that believe, is He so to you? Paul longed to depart, to be with—James? Isaiah? No, but to be with Jesus? You have some who are dear to you on earth, you have more in heaven. Perhaps you have a child, lovely here, but a cherub there. Perhaps you have a mother there, whose knees were the altar on which you laid your little hands to pray. But, thinking of Jesus, can you say,—"Whom have I in heaven but Thee? and there is none on earth I desire besides Thee?" If, then, you have thus "received Christ," what should prevent you claiming the privilege of having become a child of God? "To as many as received Him, to them, gave He power to become the sons of God."

OBEDIENCE.

Without obedience, as has well been remarked, an orthodox creed, the clearest knowledge, high confidence, much talk of Divine things, great zeal for a party, will all in vain be called in to denominate any one a believer in Christ. We must " walk in the truth."

Faith without works is as the body without the soul, there is nothing vital or operative in it. The Gospel is a doctrine according to godliness, every part of it has a practical tendency, and we are required to obey it from the heart. " Blessed are they that hear the Word of God, and *keep it*." " If ye know these things, happy are ye if ye *do* them." " Ye are my friends," says Christ, " if ye do whatsoever I command you." Thus it appears, that though He is the friend, He is also the law-giver.

We must not allow His goodness to weaken our sense of His greatness. He is the Prince as well as the Saviour. He " commands " his friends, and nothing less than obedience to his will is required of us. And our obedience must be impartial, we must do " whatsoever " he commands us. Obedience may be sincere without being perfect in the degree, but it cannot be sincere without being universal in the principle and disposition. We should be able to say with the Psalmist,—" I esteem *all* Thy commandments concerning all things to be right, and I hate *every* false way."

Thus does it appear that the believer must be characterized by good works. We do not say such good works are meritorious, for this is impossible, and the very notion subverts the Gospel of Christ. But still it is true, that though faith can alone justify the soul, works can alone justify faith, and prove it to be the operation of God.

Are you, then, dear reader, whilst relying on the promises, also striving to obey the precepts? I ask not whether your obedience is perfect, for the obedience of the holiest of men falls far short of this, but I ask whether you are sincerely and perseveringly endeavoring to do you your duty as God indicates it, and are grieved in view of your manifold delinquencies and imperfections? There is a blemish in every duty, a deficiency in every grace, a mixture in every character; it will not do, therefore, to consider those only the people of God who are free from infirmity; nor should you regard yourself as an "alien from the commonwealth of Israel," because you are conscious of numberless shortcomings and imperfections.

LOVE FOR CHRIST'S PEOPLE AND CAUSE.

"We know," says an Apostle, "that we have passed from death unto life, because we love the brethren." Thus is "brotherly-love," given as a prominent mark of grace.

What *is* this love? Is it only an attachment to those belonging to our own denomination? Evidently not. Unhappily the Christian Church is divided into sects and parties, and one of the deplorable effects of this condition is, the production of sectarian love and zeal, while there is comparative indifference to other divisions of the kingdom of the Redeemer. It is too much forgotten that Jesus said,—"They that are not against us, are for us." It is well, and perhaps natural, to feel a deep interest in our own denomination, but our love must rise above and extend beyond that. We must love all who bear the image of the Redeemer—"all who love our Lord Jesus Christ in sincerity." We must love *Christians*, and love them in spite of their differences and faults. Without intending to disparage, in the slightest degree, the importance which attaches to an orthodox faith, we cannot but regard it as painfully too true, in these latter days, that

> " With zeal we watch,
> And weigh the doctrine, while the spirit 'scapes,
> And in the carving of our cummin-seeds,
> Our metaphysical hair-splittings, fail
> To note the orbit of the star of love
> Which never sets."

If we only love those who belong to our particular branch of Zion, there is so far evidence that our religion is tinctured with unholy bigotry. It is more party-spirit than Divine love. We must extend our Christian affection to all whom we have good reason to believe have become the children of God by the regenerating influence of His Spirit, and the exercise of saving faith in His Son. God forbid that we should plead for excessive liberality in this direction. We are far from undervaluing Divine truth. It is a good thing that the heart be established with grace. The candor which regards all sentiments alike, and considers no errors as destructive, is no virtue. It is the offspring of ignorance, of insensibility, and of cold indifference. The blind do not perceive the difference of colors. The dead never dispute. Ice, as it congeals, aggregates all bodies within its reach, however heterogeneous their quality. Every virtue has certain bounds, and when it exceeds them it becomes a vice, for the last step of a virtue, and the first of a vice, are contiguous. But surely it is no unwarrantable candor to consider him a Christian, and to claim for him Christian love, whom we see professing his faith in Christ, abhorring and forsaking sin, hungering and thirsting after righteousness, diligent in approaching unto God, walking " in newness of life," and manifesting spirituality of temper, a disposition for devotion, benevolence of spirit, and deadness to the world.

As to *the cause of religion*, it, too, must be loved. Our hearts must be united to it. How may we know that this is true of us? Just as we know our regard for a person or a thing. Our attachment to anything manifests itself by our loving to hear of it, thinking much of it, speaking much of it, and delighting to remember it. We show our affection for an individual by extending to him our sympathy, feeling his interests to be our own, weeping when he weeps, and rejoicing when he rejoices. The case is the same in regard to the cause of Christ. If we love it, it will be much in our thoughts, we will strive to recommend it by our example, we will endeavor to defend it when it is assailed, we will pray, labor, and give for its success, and exult in its prosperity.

A desire to see others saved, accompanied with corresponding effort, is strong evidence of being in a gracious state. It is recorded of that eminent minister, the Rev. John Howe, that in his latter days he greatly desired to attain such a knowledge of Christ, and feel such a sense of his love, as might be a foretaste of the joys of heaven. After his death, a paper was found in his Bible recording how God had answered his prayer. One morning (and he noted the day) he awoke, his eyes swimming with tears, overwhelmed with a sense of God's goodness in shedding down his grace into the hearts of men. He never could forget the joy of these moments; they made him long still more ardently for that heaven, which, from his youth, he had panted to behold.

The Rev. Dr. Guthrie, in a sermon on the text, "The tree is known by its fruit," after specifying certain other tests of genuine piety, proceeds to say:— "Again, when you see transgressors, is it with indifference, or with somewhat of the feelings of Him who said, I saw transgressions and was grieved—rivers of water ran down mine eyes, because they keep not thy law, O Lord? Again, when you think of perishing souls, is yours the spirit of Cain, or of Christ? Can you no more stand by with folded hands to see sinners perishing than men drowning? Are you moved by such generous impulse as draws the hurrying crowd to the pool where one is sinking, and moves some brave man, at the jeopardy of life, to leap in and pluck him from the jaws of death? There is no better evidence that we have received the nature as well as the name of Christ, than an anxious wish to save lost souls, and a sympathy with the joy of angels over every sinner that is converted. Let me illustrate this by an example—a picture drawn from life.

"Years ago, and in a parish which I knew, there lived a woman notorious in the neighborhood for profane swearing, habits of drunkenness, and manners rude, coarse, as well as irreligious. She feared not God, neither regarded man, and trained up her children for the devil. One evening she happened to be within ear-shot of a preacher, and as he was emptying his quiver among the crowd, an arrow from the bow, drawn at a venture, was lodged in her heart. Remarkable example of free, sovereign, subduing grace! She was converted. Her case, as much as that of the thief on the cross, of the jailor at Philippi, of Saul on his way to Damascus, was one of instant conversion—day burst on her soul without a dawn. She hastened home. She found her family asleep, and saw in each child a never-dying soul, that her own hand had rocked into deeper, fatal slumbers. Seized with an intense desire to have them saved, she could not delay the matter till to-morrow, and so, rushing on the sleepers as if the bed beneath them had been in flames, she shook them, woke them, crying, Arise, call upon thy God! And there, at the midnight hour, with her children kneeling round her, her eyes streaming with tears, her voice trembling with emotion, did that poor mother cry to God, that he would have mercy also on them, and pluck these brands from the burning.

"Such fruit grows not in any but renewed hearts. So to feel proves what no profession can, that the same mind is in us that was in Jesus Christ. Nor is there room to doubt, that, if you bear such saintly and heavenly fruit, you are one with Him who, communicating the influences of the Spirit to his people, as the tree does its sap to the boughs, hath said, I am the vine, ye are the branches. Abide in me, and I in you."

How is it, then, dear reader, with *you* in the two particulars just noticed? Do you not feel your heart warm towards those whom you regard as partakers of the grace of eternal life? Do you not find pleasure in associating with them? Are you not prompted, as far as you are able, to bear their burdens? And do you not feel your heart rising toward God, and count yourself happy in longing and laboring for the extension of his kingdom? I ask not whether there are variations in your experience touching these points, for such variations are to be expected. I only inquire whether God, who was once to you a dream, sometimes a dream faint as the faintest vision of the night, which flits across the mind and leaves no trace, sometimes a dream of higher power and more definite form, but still at last a dream, is not now the real, abiding object of your supreme regard, and whether it is not your highest aim to please him and enjoy the light of his life-giving countenance. And can these things be true of one who is not a Christian?

Tests might be multiplied. I might tell how the Christian likes the Word of Truth, as the child it's mothers breast —likes the house of God, where the spirit of life is wont to be given, and life mingles with life, and warms and blazes—likes the Sabbath, the foretaste, the preparation of eternity, and likes prayer, the strong arm of life, the key of life, more abundant. But on these points, so plain and familiar, I need not enlarge, except to say that such a taste cannot exist in any one whose heart has not been changed by the Spirit of God. Most certainly the "carnal mind" has no such affinities and attachments.

Yield not, then, to the doubts and fears which may assail you. The sun still shines, even when covered with clouds, and you are not to question your piety because misgivings eclipse or darken your consciousness of an interest in the favor of God. Neither are you to regard your apprehensions concerning your spiritual state as unbelief. They are not so. We are, indeed, commanded to "fear, lest a promise being left us of entering into rest, any of us should seem to come short of it." Fear of failure is one method which God adopts to secure the final and complete salvation of his people. Be it yours to "hold fast the profession of your faith without wavering." The tender fruits which now grow from the new nature which you have received will gradually mature and strengthen. Though now you can but see men as trees walking, soon you will be able to look with a firm and steady gaze. Though now you tremble under temptation, soon will you be able to offer a firm resistance. Though now your peace be but as the rill that gurgles from the mountain rock, it is the promise of God that hereafter it shall "flow as a river." If, as we trust is the case, you have committed your soul to Jesus; if, realizing your guilty and ruined condition, you have cast yourself upon him as your only hope and help, saying:

"Here, Lord, I give myself away,
'Tis all that I can do;"

this is all you need do, this is all He asks you to do, and there is no good reason why you should be dejected and distressed. Your path, instead of leading you over high mountain summits, may often lead you through dark and dreary valleys, yet it is the path which God, who is too wise to err, too good to be unkind, has chosen to conduct you to heaven. Pursue that path and it will brighten as you advance. "Then shall ye know, if ye follow on to know the Lord." Live near to Christ, relying on his righteousness, and striving to imitate his example. Look not so much to your own heart as to Him who was lifted up on the cross, that whosoever believeth in him might not perish, but have everlasting life. The bitten Israelite was not healed by looking at and examining his wound, but by gazing upon the brazen serpent elevated upon the pole, neither is the Christian to expect his sanctification to advance by looking continually at his sins, but by keeping the eye of faith steadily fixed on Him who "died for our offences, and rose again for our justification."

"We have already said," remarks the

Rev. Dr. *Vinet*, " how necessary self-consideration is, and we need not repeat, but though it is impossible to contemplate our misery without being urged towards Christ, or to contemplate Jesus Christ without being recalled to a sense of our misery ; this misery is not, however, the object of saving faith, and the view of this misery cannot place in our heart the elements of life and earnests of salvation. It must even be confessed that, though powerless to save, it is able to destroy. It alternately discourages and sours, it even does both at the same time. It exhausts, and in barren regrets enervates the soul which lives on joy and hope, but dies of sadness, and the only life which remains to it in this death, is ill-humor, peevishness, murmuring and envy.

" Either Jesus Christ must be looked at incessantly, or we must look incessantly at sin. The eye, at least, if it is not blind, has no alternative, and if it is certain that we shall not lose sight of our misery by looking at Christ crucified, because this misery is, as it were, engraved upon the cross, it is equally certain that in looking at our misery, we may lose sight of Jesus Christ, because the cross is not naturally engraved on the image of our misery. An Apostle was blamed for wishing to put his hands into the wounds of his risen Master. We all concur in blaming him, and ask, why did he not rather put them into his own wounds, the wounds of his soul? But in another view, the example of Thomas should furnish us with a rule, for it is not into our own wounds, but into those of Jesus, that we ought to put our hands, and it is in this sense that we say to the class of believers whom we have in view: Look, yes look everywhere, look to the depth of your misery, but look more to Jesus Christ, at least never consent to see yourself and your sin, except through the medium of Jesus Christ, and his triumphant love."

Him on yonder cross I love,
    Naught on earth I else count dear ;
May He mine forever prove,
    Who is now so inly near.
Here I stand ; whate'er may come,
Days of sunshine or of gloom,
From this word I will not move,
Him upon the cross I love !

'Tis not hidden from my heart
    What true love must often bring ;
Want and grief have sorest smart,
    Care and scorn can sharply sting.
Nay, but if Thy will were such,
Bitterest death were not too much.
Dark though here my course may prove,
Him upon the cross I love !

Rather sorrows such as these,
    Rather love's acutest pain,
Than without Him days of ease,
    Riches false and honors vain.
Count me strange when I am true ;
What He hates I will not do ·

Sneers no more my heart can move,
Him upon the cross I love!

Know ye whence my strength is drawn,
   Fearless thus the fight to wage?
Why my heart can laugh to scorn
   Fleshly weakness, Satan's rage?
'Tis, I know, the love of Christ;
Mighty is that love unpriced.
What can grieve me, what can move?
Him upon the cross I love!

Once the eyes that now are dim
   Shall discern the changeless love,
That hath led us home to Him,
   That hath crown'd us far above.
Would to God that all below
What that love is now might know
And their hearts this word approve
Him upon the cross I love!

www.ingramcontent.com/pod-product-compliance
Lightning Source LLC
Chambersburg PA
CBHW022149090426
42742CB00010B/1436